LIFE DURING THE
REVOLUTIONARY
WAR

by Bonnie Hinman

Content Consultant
Robert J. Allison
Chair of History Department
Suffolk University

Core Library

An Imprint of Abdo Publishing
www.abdopublishing.com

www.abdopublishing.com

Published by Abdo Publishing, a division of ABDO, PO Box 398166, Minneapolis, Minnesota 55439. Copyright © 2015 by Abdo Consulting Group, Inc. International copyrights reserved in all countries. No part of this book may be reproduced in any form without written permission from the publisher. Core Library™ is a trademark and logo of Abdo Publishing.

Printed in the United States of America, North Mankato, Minnesota
092014
012015

THIS BOOK CONTAINS
RECYCLED MATERIALS

Cover Photo: North Wind Picture Archives/AP Images
Interior Photos: North Wind Picture Archives/AP Images, 1; North Wind Picture Archives, 4, 7, 8, 12, 15, 18, 23, 26, 28, 31, 33, 36, 38, 42, 45; Red Line Editorial, 16; Bettmann/Corbis, 20

Editor: Mirella Miller
Series Designer: Becky Daum

Library of Congress Control Number: 2014944212

Cataloging-in-Publication Data
Hinman, Bonnie.
 Life during the Revolutionary War / Bonnie Hinman.
   p. cm. -- (Daily life in US history)
 ISBN 978-1-62403-628-6 (lib. bdg.)
 Includes bibliographical references and index.
 1. United States--Revolution, 1775-1783--Social aspects--Juvenile literature.   2. United States--Social life and customs--1775-1783--Juvenile literature.   I. Title.
 973.3--dc23

                                                    2014944212

CONTENTS

CHAPTER ONE

THE UNITED STATES IS BORN

t's April 18, 1775, in Charlestown, Massachusetts. A rattling outside your bedroom window wakes you up. You tiptoe to the window. The moon is bright, and you can see two men across the street. A brown horse dances between the men, its hooves striking the cobblestones on the street.

British troops entered Boston, Massachusetts, in the 1770s to enforce taxes and laws put in place by Great Britain.

The Thirteen Colonies

If you lived in Massachusetts during the Revolutionary War (1775–1783), you might have seen Paul Revere heading north on his horse. Revere is known for his ride to warn of British troops. European settlers had lived in North America for more than 150 years by the time Revere made his famous ride. From 1607 to 1775, Great Britain ruled 13 colonies on what is now the East Coast of the United States.

Life in the colonies was never easy. Colonists grew food, built homes, made clothing, and did many other jobs they had never done before. But by the mid-1700s, colonial life was becoming easier. Colonists still had to work hard, but most people

Paul Revere

Two of Paul Revere's friends rowed him across the Charles River from Boston to Charlestown. Then Revere borrowed a horse and rode to the nearby towns of Lexington and Concord. He warned military leaders that British troops were marching toward their towns. The American military leaders prepared to fight the British troops.

Native Americans and Europeans trade furs aboard a ship.

had food and a home. Some colonists even became rich.

The 13 colonies were very different from one another. Each of the colonies had its own government. The colonies traded with one another but were not officially connected.

Middle colonies, such as New York, had bigger farms to produce their own products. The British taxes and laws did not affect their lives as much.

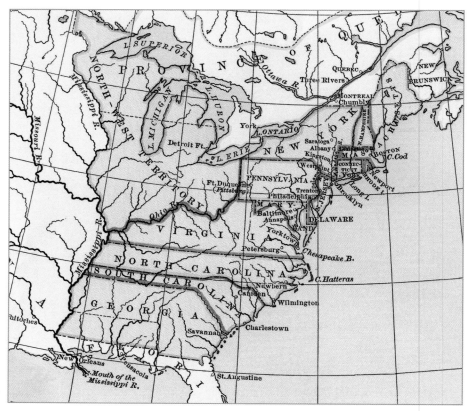

The 13 Colonies

This map shows the 13 colonies. The North had rocky ground and mountain ranges. The South had flat areas with large fields. Some colonies had large farms, while others did not. Thinking about the geography of these areas, can you tell why colonies specialized in certain crops?

Southern colonies, such as Virginia, had huge plantations. Tobacco was their biggest cash crop. Thousands of slaves worked on the plantations. Slaves were taken from their homes in Africa. They were brought to the colonies to work.

Continental Congresses

Trouble began brewing between the colonies and Great Britain around 1763. Great Britain claimed the 13 colonies as its own. Many colonists wanted more independence. King George III and the British Parliament forced new taxes and trade restrictions on the colonies. Most colonists wanted to remain connected to Great Britain, but they did not like the new taxes.

In 1774 and 1775, a group of delegates met in Philadelphia, Pennsylvania. These meetings were called the First and Second Continental Congresses. Some delegates thought it was time to stand up to King George and the

PERSPECTIVES
Loyalists

American colonists who remained loyal to Great Britain made a difficult decision and suffered for that choice. Called Loyalists, they were often targeted by other colonists as enemies because they did not support the war. Loyalists' houses might be burned or seized by the Patriots. Patriots were colonists who supported the Revolutionary War.

British Parliament. But most delegates wanted the British to change the laws that hurt the colonists.

Some delegates went to Great Britain to talk to Parliament and King George about removing some of the laws. But in the meantime, the delegates also ordered US general George Washington to build an army.

Declaring War

When Great Britain did not change the laws, the delegates declared independence on July 4, 1776. King George did not let the colonies go without a fight. The Revolutionary War raged for seven years.

However, regular life did not stop during war. Even as battles were fought, most children still learned to read and write. Parents tended their farms and businesses and went to church on Sunday.

Many men, women, and children also made great sacrifices, including their lives. But to most Americans, it was worth it. They were proud to say they were citizens of the new United States of America.

Letters were the only way to communicate over long distances during the Revolutionary War. Delegate John Adams wrote letters to his wife, Abigail, while he was meeting in the Continental Congress. The following is an excerpt from a letter he wrote to Abigail on July 3, 1776:

> *The Second Day of July 1776 will be the most memorable Epocha, in the History of America. I am apt to believe that it will be celebrated, by succeeding Generations, as the great anniversary Festival. It ought to be commemorated, as the Day of Deliverance by solemn Acts of Devotion to God Almighty. It ought to be solemnized with Pomp and Parade, with Shews, Games, Sports, Guns, Bells, Bonfires and Illuminations from one End of this Continent to the other from this Time forward forever more.*

Source: The Adams Papers: Adams Family Correspondence. *Ed. L. H. Butterfield. New York: Atheneum, 1965. Print. 30.*

Consider Your Audience

Adams's letter uses different language from what we use today. How could you adapt Adams's words for your friends or classmates? Write a blog post giving this same information to the new audience. What is the most effective way to get your point across? How is the language you use different from Adams's? Why?

CHAPTER TWO

HOME SWEET HOME

Much of colonists' everyday lives during the Revolutionary War depended on where they lived. Houses were especially different across the colonies. Houses in the northern colonies, such as Massachusetts and Connecticut, were built to keep the heat inside throughout the cold winters. The houses had low ceilings and small windows. Northern

Log cabins were built in the western frontier areas of Pennsylvania, Kentucky, and Virginia.

houses often had a fireplace in the middle of the house so several rooms could be heated at once.

In southern colonies, such as Georgia and the Carolinas, ceilings were high and windows were large. This helped keep the houses cool during the long, hot summers. Chimney stacks were on the outside walls of houses. Unlike in the North, kitchens were often built in separate buildings. This kept the heat of cooking out of the main house.

Slaves in the South lived in slaves' quarters on the plantations. These

PERSPECTIVES
Native American Homes

Thousands of Native Americans lived in the United States long before colonists arrived. They used their surroundings to survive. Different Native American groups had different kinds of homes. Some lived in long houses with shared cooking and sleeping areas. Many Native Americans in the southern colonies lived in small houses surrounded by bean and cornfields. Another tribe built four long buildings in a square surrounding a center field area.

Specialty stores became more common during the Revolutionary War era. People could buy dry goods or food at the stores.

quarters were several small wooden shacks built near the main house. Dirt floors and small windows were common. Some shacks did not have any windows.

Colonial Food

As important as houses were to the colonists, most colonists were more concerned about food and clothing. Early colonists spent most of their time finding or producing food.

By the Revolutionary War, many colonists spent less time directly producing food and clothing. As the

Eating Out during the Revolutionary War

Eating out was not the fun experience for Revolutionary Era families that it is today. The food was not very good at the taverns and coffeehouses. British money was the currency used most often in colonial days. It was divided into the following denominations:

British Money	Symbol	Equal to:
1 pound	£	20 shillings
1 shilling	s	12 pennies
240 pennies	d	1 pound

If a tavern meal cost 1s 3d and you needed to feed your family of four, how much money would you need? How many 2s meals could you buy with 1£?

population grew, colonists began to specialize their skills. A barrel-maker no longer needed to make his own cloth or grow all of his own food too. Instead, he sold his barrels and used that money to buy goods from other merchants or farmers.

British settlers liked beef. Many cows were in the colonies by 1776. Pork was also popular. Pigs could run free and feed themselves until the colonists needed them for food. Colonists also traded pork and beef with other countries.

Fish were a staple of New Englanders' diets as well. Any colonist living along a body of water ate fish often. Colonists also traded salted codfish. This became a staple in the diets of slaves in the Caribbean.

Many vegetables grew in North America that the colonists had not eaten in their former homes. Some of these included pumpkins, green peppers, corn, and sweet potatoes.

Wealthy colonists served lavish meals to show off their success. They entertained at dinner parties with dozens of different foods on their tables. Food for less

American-Made Fabric

During the Revolutionary War, colonists boycotted all British-made goods. Women were the biggest reason the boycotts were successful. Women refused to purchase any kind of fabric imported from Great Britain. They organized all-day sewing events and wore clothing made of homespun cloth. Even wealthy women, such as Deborah Franklin, wife of politician Benjamin Franklin, made her family's clothing to show support for the colonies.

Colonial women increased their own production of fabric and other goods to meet the demand for cloth.

wealthy colonists depended on what they could afford. Most meals included stews, puddings, and bread. Dinner at a farmer's home may have had more variety since he grew his own food.

Clothing

The type of clothing the colonists wore depended on their social class. Wealthy colonists used their clothing to let others know how successful they were. They often wore many layers of expensive cloth.

Working class people wore clothing suited to their jobs. They wore fewer layers. Their clothing was usually made of homespun cloth. This was a coarse fabric woven from wool and flax.

Food, clothing, and housing were the essentials of life during the Revolutionary War era, but they were not the only important things. Once those basics were met, parents turned to providing education for their children.

FURTHER EVIDENCE

There is quite a bit of information about colonial clothing in Chapter Two. If you could pick out the main point of the chapter, what would it be? What evidence was given to support that point? Visit the website below to learn more about colonial dress. Choose a quote from the website that relates to the chapter. Does this quote support the author's main point? Does it make a new point? Write a few sentences explaining how the quote you found relates to this chapter.

Williamsburg's Homespun Ball
www.mycorelibrary.com/revolutionary-war

CHAPTER THREE

SCHOOL DAYS

Children learned reading, then writing, and then arithmetic in school. Learning to write came several years after reading. Arithmetic was learned even later. It was not unusual for a five-year-old to learn to read but not learn to write until he or she was seven or eight years old.

During the Revolutionary War, boys and girls learned how to read and write at dame schools.

Dame Schools

Children who lived on farms miles from any village or town were taught to read by their parents. Many children who lived in villages or towns went to dame schools. A village woman was paid a small fee for teaching children to read in her kitchen. She tended to her own family and performed other chores while teaching.

Depending on where a child lived, the only schooling he or she received was a few years at dame school. Boys sometimes went on to study at schools taught by schoolmasters. Girls were rarely allowed to attend those schools.

Writing Schools

Children were taught to read before they learned how to write. Reading was a skill everyone needed in order to read the Bible. By the time of the Revolution, parents saw their children needed to learn more than how to read. Penmanship was very important. Children, and even some adults, went to special writing schools to learn how to write words properly. Many Americans believed an education would help the United States become a strong nation.

Children of all ages sat on benches in one-room schoolhouses.

However, this began to change around the time of the Revolutionary War. Citizens of the newly formed United States needed to be informed so they could understand the new changes happening.

Changing Times

More girls between the ages of six and eight were allowed to learn to read and write. But girls were encouraged to only learn the basics of reading and writing. They were expected to be too busy working at home to have time to use any other skills.

A schoolmaster, or teacher, often had dozens of students from age five to age twelve. The teacher was usually a strict man. Students often said their lessons aloud, which made the schoolroom noisy. The schoolroom only had benches to sit on.

Slave Schools

Slaves in some of the colonies were taught to read so they could read the Bible. Missionaries sometimes did the teaching, but often a slave owner or his wife would teach slaves to read. Slaves were never taught to write, although a few taught themselves. Owners believed slaves who could write might write a note pretending to be their owner and free themselves. A slave who could read and write was seen as dangerous. That slave could use these skills to get other slaves to rebel against their owners. In the years after the Revolutionary War, many states did not allow slaves to be taught to read.

Boarding School

Some children of wealthy families went to boarding schools. Many Southern children had tutors who lived on the plantations. A tutor would teach the owner's children and sometimes the neighbor's children.

As the Revolutionary War approached and passed, children were taught skills that would be useful in whatever business or trade they planned to begin as an adult. Arithmetic became more important. Businesspeople, as well as farmers and other

PERSPECTIVES
Plantation Tutor

Attending school on a southern plantation was more pleasant than attending most other schools. Philip Fithian kept a journal of the year he spent as a tutor on the Robert Carter plantation in Virginia. Fithian's eight students ranged from ages five to seventeen. Fithian taught reading, writing, and arithmetic. The boys also studied Latin and Greek. Fithian wrote that school was often interrupted by dancing and music lessons given by other instructors. School was frequently canceled for picnics, balls, and other entertainment.

Sometimes children of wealthy families traveled back to Great Britain to attend school.

tradesmen, needed to keep track of the money in their businesses.

Revolutionary War–era children had more chances to go to school and learn than before. But the children of wealthy parents still had the best education.

EXPLORE ONLINE

The focus in Chapter Three was on schooling during the Revolutionary War. The website below focuses on the same subject. As you know, every source is different. How is the information given on the website different from the information in this chapter? What information is the same? How do the two sources present information differently? What can you learn from this website?

Education in the Revolutionary Era
www.mycorelibrary.com/revolutionary-war

CHAPTER FOUR

A DAY'S WORK

The first American colonists were farmers. They had to eat, and there were no grocery stores. Colonists grew their own food and made everything else they needed to live. As the years went by and the colonies grew, farmers began to branch out. Many farmers had other businesses. Sometimes they practiced a trade or skill they had done before coming to America. But often, they learned a new

As colonies grew, people learned new skills to help their communities grow too.

skill that was needed in their community. A farmer who learned carpentry when helping his neighbors build their houses could become a full-time builder. His carpentry skills became more important to the community than what he could produce as a farmer.

Apprentices

Early America never had enough workers. The apprentice system helped fill that gap. Young boys were apprenticed to a craftsman who owned a shop or business. Boys were usually between 12 and 14 years old when their families sent them to live with a man who taught them his trade in exchange for their unskilled labor. The craftsmen were called masters and agreed to provide food, clothing, a bed, and sometimes schooling in the evenings for their apprentices.

Apprentices did not have an easy life. They sometimes had to work in a trade they did not like. Some masters were kind and did all they could to teach their apprentices. Others were much more

The apprentice system produced thousands of craftsmen to help build and maintain the colonies.

concerned with the free labor and made their apprentices work very hard.

Many Trades

A few of the trades in America included tailor, miller, silversmith, hat-maker, weaver, and eyeglasses seller. At the time of the Revolutionary War, there were 35 different trades on a list. Other trades may have not been mentioned. Professional jobs existed too. These were lawyers, doctors, and ministers.

Plantation Workers

Large southern plantations were similar to small towns. The people living there did everything for themselves. Luxuries came from Great Britain and other countries, but daily necessities were made right on the plantation.

Slaves provided the labor for almost every job done on a plantation. Slaves had no freedom and were often separated from their families. They could be sold to another

Most slaves worked in the tobacco, cotton, and rice fields.

owner at any time. House slaves were servants in the homes. But slaves also learned to do more skilled jobs, such as blacksmithing, barrel making, and weaving. A plantation could not function without its slaves.

During the Revolutionary War, some slaves joined the armies of both sides. Many fled their homes in search of freedom. If a plantation owner and his family moved to escape an oncoming army, they often left their slaves behind to fight for themselves.

Women's Roles

Most women did not officially work at jobs during the Revolutionary War time period. But they did many of the same jobs as men, serving as helpers. Farm women could do almost everything their husbands did. When their husbands left the farms to join the army during the war, the women took over running the farms. Wealthier women had the responsibility of running large households. These households had many servants or slaves to supervise.

Children Working

Children also worked. Girls usually helped their mothers by doing chores. For many girls, their first chore was watching their younger brothers and sisters. A girl as young as four years old might care for her siblings. Boys worked with their fathers on farms, in shops, or in workshops. When very young, the boys fed chickens, swept shops, and ran errands.

There was a lot of work to be done during the Revolutionary War years. Some work was made harder because of the war. But children still played, and adults still found time to join in the games and go to parties.

CHAPTER FIVE

TIME FOR FUN

There was plenty of hard work during the Revolutionary War, but children and adults both found time to enjoy themselves. Colonial children played dozens of games. Young men liked having footraces and wrestling. Horse racing was also popular among wealthier men. Soldiers played cards and sometimes gambled. Businessmen often met at taverns to talk about business and politics.

Colonial children did not have many toys, but they played outside and made up games.

Wealthy colonists regularly attended balls and dances in big cities.

Meeting Up

Attending church services on Sunday was a social event. Colonists also attended other church activities, such as revivals and holiday celebrations. Church members helped each other when a family suffered a tragedy such as a house fire.

Wives and older daughters of wealthy colonists held teas and other afternoon gatherings. During the Revolutionary War, some wealthy women met to help American soldiers. Some collected money and others met to spin yarn for clothing.

Farm women had less time to socialize. They managed to get together sometimes to make quilts or sew clothing for soldiers.

Slaves had very little time for fun. Their lives were hard. However, they did enjoy themselves with music and dance. Music and dance was inspired by traditions from their homelands.

Drumming

Drums and drummer boys played an important role in the Revolutionary War. The drums beat out many different rhythms to tell soldiers what to do. This was important, since even shouted commands might not be heard in the noise of battle.

Published Books

By the time of the Revolutionary War, most colonists could read. They took advantage of the increasing number of books available to them. Almost all books were about practical subjects, such as farming.

Thousands of pamphlets, or small books, were published in the years before and during the Revolutionary War. Pamphlets were cheap to

Phillis Wheatley

Most slaves faced a lifetime of hard work. But a few slaves were bought by caring families. Phillis Wheatley was owned by the Wheatley family. The Wheatleys allowed Phillis to learn to read and write. Soon, she was reading Greek and Latin and began writing poetry. Phillis traveled to London, where she got support to print a book of poetry. Wheatley's book was a success both in Great Britain and America.

print. The most famous pamphlet published was Thomas Paine's *Common Sense*. The pamphlet spelled out the reasons for America declaring independence from Great Britain.

A Time of Change

The Revolutionary War caused some of the biggest changes America had ever seen. Every colony and every colonist was affected by the war. Yet Americans still lived their daily lives. Those normal experiences and events were lived against a backdrop of uncertainty. The colonists did not know America would win the war, and with it, a future of independence.

Thomas Paine's famous pamphlet *Common Sense* was published in 1776. The following excerpt explains why it was important to declare freedom from Great Britain:

> *Youth is the seed time of good habits, as well in nations as in individuals. It might be difficult, if not impossible, to form the Continent into one government half a century hence. The vast variety of interests, occasioned by an increase of trade and population, would create confusion. Colony would be against colony. Each being able might scorn each other's assistance; and while the proud and the foolish gloried in their little distinctions, the wise would lament, that the union had not been formed before. Wherefore, the PRESENT TIME is the TRUE TIME for establishing it.*

Source: Thomas Paine. Common Sense. Philadelphia: W. and T. Bradford, 1776. Print. 28.

What's the Big Idea?

Read this excerpt carefully. What is Thomas Paine trying to convince the colonists to do? What evidence is used to support his point? Come up with a few sentences showing how Paine uses two or three pieces of evidence to support his main point.

When farmers left to join the war, their wives and children were left to take care of the farms. Farmers' wives had to take on their husbands' duties, and keep up their own.

5:00 a.m.

Mix five loaves of bread and set to rise. Feed the baby. Throw down hay for the horses. Milk the cow and let the chickens out of the coop.

7:00 a.m.

Feed the toddlers bread and milk for breakfast. Add wood to the fire to heat the oven for baking. Bake five loaves of bread. Pick beans from the garden while the bread bakes.

9:00 a.m.

Feed the baby again. Mend the toddlers' clothes. Take the bread out of the oven to cool. Put a pot of stew on the fire to cook for supper. Take the children along to work on replacing a fence post the cow broke down. Pick blackberries on the way back to the house.

11:00 a.m.
Roll out crusts for two blackberry pies. Put the pies in the oven. Cut out two shirts and three vests to sew for husband.

12:00 p.m.
Feed the toddlers milk and cheese. Put them in bed for a nap. Shell beans from the garden and add to the stew. Pull weeds from the garden while the children nap.

1:00 p.m.
Collect eggs from the chicken coop. Begin sewing the shirts and vests.

3:00 p.m.
Take one pie and a loaf of bread to husband's father, who lives one mile (1.6 km) away. Carry the baby while the toddlers walk alongside.

5:00 p.m.
Feed the baby again. Milk the cow again. Set the milk to cool for churning into butter in the morning. Feed the chickens corn. Put the horses back in the shed.

7:00 p.m.
Eat the stew and blackberry pie with the toddlers. Put all the children to bed. Wash the dishes and sweep the kitchen floor. Write a letter to husband.

8:00 p.m.
Read the Bible and go to bed.

STOP AND THINK

Take a Stand

When the Continental Congresses met in 1774 and 1775, the delegates had different ideas about how to persuade Great Britain to leave the colonies to govern themselves. Find one of these ideas in Chapter One. Why do you think this is a good idea? Write a short essay explaining your opinion. Make sure to give reasons for your opinion, and facts and details that support those reasons.

You Are There

Chapter Two describes the homes, food, and clothing that colonists had. Pretend you live back then. What kind of a house would you live in? What would you grow in your garden? If you had a farm, what animals would you raise? How would you feel about wearing the many different layers of clothing some colonists wore?

Why Do I Care?

Most children had to work a lot harder in colonial days. Do kids today have to do any of the same kinds of work? Write a list of jobs that you have to do today that are similar to the ones kids did then. Write another list of jobs that are different from what you might do today.

Say What?

Studying the Revolutionary War can mean learning a lot of new vocabulary. Find five words in the book that you've never heard before. Use a dictionary to find out what they mean. Then write the meanings in your own words, and use each new word in a sentence.

GLOSSARY

boycott
to refuse to buy, use, or participate in something as a way of protesting

delegate
a person chosen or voted to act for others

diplomat
a person who works for his or her government in other countries

imported
brought into a country to be sold there

pamphlet
a small, thin book with no cover or with a paper cover

penmanship
quality or style of handwriting

staple
a chief food or product in constant use or demand

trade
an occupation that often requires manual or mechanical skill

LEARN MORE

Books

Cohn, Scotti. *Liberty's Children: Stories of Eleven Revolutionary War Children*. Guilford, CT: Globe Pequot Press, 2004.

Gregory, Josh. *The Revolutionary War*. New York: Scholastic, 2011.

Roberts, Cokie. *Founding Mothers: Remembering the Ladies*. New York: HarperCollins, 2014.

Websites

To learn more about Daily Life in US History, visit **booklinks.abdopublishing.com**. These links are routinely monitored and updated to provide the most current information available.

Visit **www.mycorelibrary.com** for free additional tools for teachers and students.

INDEX

ABOUT THE AUTHOR

Bonnie Hinman has more than 30 nonfiction books published. Bonnie lives in Joplin, Missouri, with her husband, Bill, and near her children and five grandchildren.